Your Six-Week Guide to a Successful Business

The Kingdom Entrepreneur Devotional

Leadership Strategies and Prayers, for Increase, Multiplication and Marketplace Impact.

Andrew & Mona Hanna

Ark House Press
arkhousepress.com

© 2022 Andrew & Mona Hanna

All rights reserved. Apart from any fair dealing for the purpose of study, research, criticism, or review, as permitted under the Copyright Act, no part may be reproduced by any process without written permission.

Unless otherwise stated, all Scriptures are taken from the New International Translation (Holy Bible. Copyright© 1996, 2004, 2007, 2013 by Tyndale House Foundation. Used by permission of Tyndale House Publishers Inc., Carol Stream, Illinois 60188. All rights reserved.)

Some names and identifying details have been changed to protect the privacy of individuals.

Cataloguing in Publication Data:
Title: The Kingdom Entrepreneur Devotional
ISBN: 9780645411799 (pbk)
Subjects: Business; Finance; Christian Living;
Other Authors/Contributors: Hanna, Andrew; Hanna, Mona

Design by initiateagency.com

Is your business struggling, or not reaching its maximum potential? Then *The Kingdom Entrepreneur Devotional* will change the direction of your business.

Many business entrepreneurs struggle in their daily Christian walk with God, especially when it comes to prayer and spending time with God. It can be that their business takes so much time out of their day that when they come to sit down and spend time with God, they don't know where to start. This can be because someone is chasing them up for something, they have to follow up a loose end from yesterday, or there are some leadership issues they must deal with right away at work.

Some of these examples may describe what is holding you back from spending more time in prayer, and yes, the struggle is real. You definitely are not alone! Business owners are some of the most time-poor people on the planet…

As business owners for over 20 years, as well as being parents and pastors, we've personally encountered this struggle and met others that are on the same journey – regardless of denomination or geographical location.

So what is the spiritual condition of our Kingdom entrepreneurs today? Many of them are feeling stuck in their spiritual journey, living off other people's spirituality, tired- physically, spiritually and emotionally. Busyness is keeping them from being intentional in pursing Jesus, and many struggle to put a stop on a life that is always on the run.

The bottom line is that many of us have a relationship with Jesus that is somewhat underdeveloped. We can talk to God, or even at God, but we don't wait to actually listen and hear what He has to say. God wants to reach the world through us, so this is actually considered to be a global spiritual crisis.

The purpose of this guided prayer and devotional is to introduce to you an opportunity to make time during your busy schedule for spiritual discipline.

This devotional provides a structured way to spend time with God, to pray and devote time and thought into how we as Kingdom entrepreneurs can release God's supernatural power and anointing into your office and the marketplace around you.

How to use this devotional

A guided devotional prophetic prayer and journal provides every entrepreneur with a flexible structure for their time spent with God. Our prayer is that the moment you dive into this devotional, you will be able to adapt to the unique demands of the season you are in and be able to make a regular time and place to spend in God's presence. What works for one person may not work for the other, and what worked before with you may not work now according to the circumstances you are in. But God sees this, so in using this devotional, please allow for grace to be the foundation of the way you journey it out.

We have, both as a married couple and Kingdom entrepreneurs, prayed over this book before it went to print and have spoken words of life and abundance over you. Yes you!! We have prayed for the supernatural abundant favour and blessings of God to overwhelm your business and produce fruit for His glory.

We declare Genesis 12:2-3 over you:

> "I will make you into a great nation and **I will bless you**; I will make your name great, and you will be a blessing. I will bless those who bless you, and whoever curses you I will curse; and all peoples on earth will be blessed through you."

The Kingdom Entrepreneur Devotional also includes a 6-week guide of praying powerful, prophetic prayers.

1. Take a moment to stay still in His presence

Each day will begin with a time of stillness and silence. The dedicated two minutes helps the entrepreneur stop their daily routine/activity and turn their attention to spending time in the presence of their Heavenly Father. This is inspired by these scriptures:

> "Be still before the Lord and wait patiently before Him." (Psalm 37:7)

> "Be still and know that I am God." (Psalm 46:10)

These scriptures clearly show us that we must choose to enter into His Holy presence, to enter the Holy of Holies and rest in His ultimate love. So basically, we begin and end each daily devotional prayer with a moment of silence where we recognise and rest in the love of our Heavenly Father.

You may not be familiar with this, and that's totally fine, but our busy lives are full of noise and distraction. Therefore this time spent with God alone may be the most challenging, but also the most rewarding time, once you've been able to establish it as a good habit.

Below are a few guidelines to help you begin entering into that place of stillness before the Lord:

- ♛ Settle in a comfortable and quiet place and take a few deep breaths, allowing yourself to inhale and exhale slowly.
- ♛ Place your mobile on Do Not Disturb because ideally, your are in a meeting with the King of Kings, and you do not want to be interrupted. Of course, this is a personal choice, but you don't want to be distracted in this time.
- ♛ Begin with a simple prayer inviting the presence of God into your workspace, lounge, or office. Express your desire to spend time with God. A few ideas are: *Abba, Father,* or *I invite our Holy presence,* or *Here I am Lord,* or *My heart is open to hear from you.*
- ♛ When distractions come your way, entrust them in the hands of God and re-align your thoughts back into this moment in His presence.

Give yourself lots of grace in this moment, as entering the presence of God simply means that you are allowing God to be the centre of your life, hence you choose to let go of your own agenda and surrender your will to His will during this time. Once you allow for this to happen, you will begin to experience a gradual transformation in your life. You will notice that you will choose a moment of silence before you come to open an important email, start driving, or even before making a major decision.

2. Scripture Reading

On some days there may be more than one scripture reading. The scriptures selected are recommended to be read out loud as there will be some words/phrases in the scripture that will stand out to you. If the Holy Spirit asks you to linger on to the scripture for longer, please do so. Allow the Holy Spirit to guide you and be attentive to what the Holy Spirit is bringing your attention to.

3. Devotional Thought

The devotional thoughts are comprised of a variety of Kingdom entrepreneurial concepts. As with the scriptures, please read these devotionals carefully and prayerfully, as some of these will speak straight into your life and give you great context as to where the scripture reading came from.

4. Prayer

Written prayers are such a powerful supplement to our devotional life, especially the ones in this book. It's a great way to start your day with a powerful prophetic declaration prayer, or you may simply want to just use these prayers as a guide to pray your own prayers.

5. Questions and Reflections (Things to consider)

Each daily devotion offers you an opportunity to critically think and reflect on how this prayer and devotion can help you move forward in your business journey. There are extra pages attached to make it helpful for you to write out your answers/extra thoughts/prayers, and so on.

6. The Holy Spirit's whisper to me today

Every day there is an opportunity to take time at the end of the devotional to hear what the Holy Spirit is communicating to you. Write it down as you see God's promises, as these spoken whispers come to pass. It will be great to reflect on this after a year, or a few years, and see what God has said, and how it has come to pass.

This is personally one of our favourite parts of the devotional, as we have experienced the power in writing what God communicates. One of the most powerful ways to know how God will move in your future is to see how He miraculously moved in your past.

Once you have completed this devotional, we pray and believe that you will experience something supernatural and new in your life, your leadership skills, your business and your workplace.

Blessings and love,
Andrew & Mona Hanna

WEEK 1, DAY 1

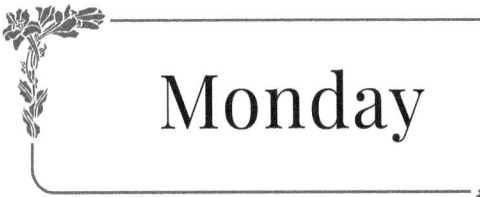

Monday

God will Open Doors in your favour

**Begin by taking a moment to stay still in God's presence.
Holy Spirit come, I turn my attention to you.**

Scripture Readings

Isaiah 45:1-3

"Thus says the Lord to His anointed Cyrus, whose right hand I have held - to subdue nations before him and loose the armour of Kings, to open before him the double doors, so that the gates will not shut: 'I will go before you and make the crooked places straight; I will break in pieces the gates of bronze and cut the bars of iron. I will give you the treasures of darkness and hidden riches in secret places, that you may know that I the Lord, who call you by your name, am the God of Israel".

Also read Isaiah 49:1-3

Devotional thought:

Every leader has a vision and wants their life to count before God. Every Christian leader feels as though everything they do matters to God and that's why they get this deep sense of feeling satisfied from their work. Some assignments of a Christian leader are found in Isaiah 49:1-3

> A leader is called from his mother's womb (vs. 1)
> A leader is gifted with certain gifts and resources (vs. 2)
> A leader is supernaturally protected by God (vs. 2)
> A leader is given a particular divine assignment (vs. 2)
> A leader is ordained to reflect God's glory (vs. 3)

With all of this being said, God then opens doors, and not normal doors, but double doors! He gives treasures of darkness and shows you hidden riches in secret places. The only requirement for these amazing things to happen is that you must speak it, believe it and declare it. Let's Pray...

Prayer:

Father, I glorify you because you, Lord, are all powerful and mighty. My heart is full of gratitude for you have called me a leader from my mothers womb. Thank you because I am gifted with heavenly resources. Tthank you for your supernatural

protection; thank you for the divine assignment you have me on, and thank you for ordaining me to reveal your glory.
I feel your presence and affection and your hand holding me. Subdue nations before me, Father. Give me nations for your sake. Subdue all forces of wickedness before me.
Open before me double doors, doors that I would never expect; doors that are double in payment for all of the closed doors I have encountered before.
Open all the gates for me that need to be opened and close the ones that need to be closed.
Go before me in all things and help me to see you going before me.
Make the crooked places in my life straight.
Release every blessing to me that has previously been held back from me.
Make known to me treasures that have been hidden from me in the dark.
Release riches to me that have been kept in secret places.
Help me to understand that you have called me by my name. You know me and you love me; I matter to you so much. Help me to know that you are the God of Israel. I pray this in your mighty name Jesus, Amen.

Things to Consider:

What are you placing before God today that you need His help on?

What are some of the visions you have for your workplace?

How are you aligning your mindset to believe what God says about you?

Take a moment to ask the Holy Spirit how He would like you to allocate resources entrusted to you as a leader to build His kingdom here on earth.

....

....

WEEK 1, DAY 2

Tuesday

A Heavenly Revelation for your Leadership

**Begin by taking a moment to stay still in God's presence.
Holy Spirit come, I turn my attention to you.**

Scripture Reading:

Galatians 2:2

"I went there because God revealed to me that I should go."

Also read Exodus 2:1-4:31

Devotional thought:

Moses was an inspirational leader. We see his journey in Exodus and the way God used him to lead the Israelites out of Egypt and the bondage they were in. God prepared Moses over a period of time. It did not happen in a day, or at a certain event- there was a process and God lead Moses through it.

Before Moses, there were also other significant men that God worked on to develop their leadership:

- ♛ Noah waited 120 years before it began to rain.
- ♛ Abraham waited 25 long years for a son.
- ♛ Joseph waited 14 years in prison, even though he hadn't committed any crimes.
- ♛ Job waited 60-70 years for God's justice and restoration.

Preparation time for a leader is crucial, but more important than the goal we wait for is the process and the work God does within us while we are waiting for our promise to be fulfilled. Waiting matures us, gives us perspective, broadens and deepens our understanding. This test of time is what determines if we can endure a time of unfruitful preparation and indicates if we can seize any given opportunity at the same time, or not.

Devotional Prayer:

Thank you Father for your Spirit that is my helper and counsellor. You are always there and available. Father, lead me in the way that I should go. Make my steps firm in you, Father. Guide me and take me to the places where you want me to

go. Remove blockages from my way. Open the right doors before me, and make the way clear before me.
Help me in this time of development and guide me through the process. Give me perspective and mature me for the things you are preparing me for.
Thank you for the spirit of Wisdom and Revelation that you have imparted within me. With this gift, help me to discern the way of success and the way of destruction. I pray for specific direction today, in Jesus mighty name I pray, Amen.

Things to consider:

In a time of waiting, consider three fruitful things that God can birth to ensure that you are on a successful journey towards your destiny:

What steps are you taking in the waiting to get to your promised land?

What area(s) do you need revelation in today? How can the Holy Spirit help you today?

What areas do you feel you need wisdom and discernment in?

....
....
....
....
....
....
....

WEEK 1, DAY 3

Wednesday

The Power of Encouragement & Prayer

**Begin by taking a moment to stay still in God's presence.
Holy Spirit come, I turn my attention to you.**

Scripture readings:

2 Thessalonians 1:11-12

"We keep on praying for you, that our God will make you worthy of the life to which he called you. And we pray that God, by His power, will fulfil all your good intentions and faithful deeds. Then everyone will give honour to the name of our Lord Jesus because of you."

2 Thessalonians 1:3-6

"We ought always to thank God for you, brothers and sisters, and rightly so, because your faith is growing more and more, and the love all of you have for one another is increasing. Therefore, among God's churches we boast about your perseverance and faith in all the persecutions and trials you are enduring.

All this is evidence that God's judgment is right, and as a result you will be counted worthy of the kingdom of God, for which you are suffering. God is just: He will pay back trouble to those who trouble you."

Devotional thought:

Everyone needs encouragement and prayer. It is the oxygen of their soul, and everyone excels with it. Paul knew the secrets on how to encourage and boast about his people, so he included that in the letter to the Thessalonians that was sent all over Asia, and it is so valid right now to leaders in this day and age.

Good leaders generously hand out encouragement. It's a great investment; it costs very little to affirm others, yet it pays great dividends.

Paul teaches us a few things about encouraging our team and our people. Encouragement must be personal (to the individual), directed (towards what you appreciate about them), and purposeful (motivating them towards another goal for them to achieve).

Devotional Prayer:

Father, we thank you for your power that is within us, enabling and empowering me to live a life worthy of my calling, for the glory of your name.

Help me to become the great leader you have called me to be. Thank you for giving me the courage and boldness to encourage others on my team. I pray that this encouragement brings forth great fruit.

Even if I have feelings of inadequacy or unworthiness, you give me the opportunity to come boldly into your presence to receive your worthiness and adequacy. When I come humbly into your presence and seek you, you divinely fill me with your grace and sufficiency to enable me to fulfil my calling. You alone can make me worthy of the life which you have called me to. Thank you, Father, that my effectiveness in your calling doesn't depend on my abilities. In your grace, impart your power and anointing within me. Make me a vessel of your glory so that those who see my works will look past me and be drawn to you. In Jesus mighty name I pray, Amen.

Things to consider:

Who do you feel in your workplace requires a bit of encouragement to motivate them to do more in your business? What actions are you taking to encourage those around you?

What active steps are you taking to achieve your vision by serving your team through encouragement?

Allow the Holy Spirit to speak to you in this area and write it down below.

....

....

WEEK 1, DAY 4

Keeping my eyes fixed.

**Begin by taking a moment to stay
still in God's presence.
Holy Spirit come, I turn my attention to you.**

Scripture readings:

2 Corinthians 4:16-18

"Therefore we do not lose heart. Though outwardly we are wasting away, yet inwardly we are being renewed day by day. For our light and momentary troubles are achieving for us an eternal glory that far outweighs them all. So we fix our eyes not on what is seen, but on what is unseen, since what is seen is temporary, but what is unseen is eternal."

Devotional thought:

As leaders, we must paint a perspective for others. Leadership is more about the way we see things than our gifting. We may be so gifted in so many areas, but Paul clarifies so clearly that the importance of the eternal realm is far more important than the visible one. Through the visible, Paul invites us to never lose heart and reminds us that our struggles are what develop us.

Devotional Prayer:

Thank you, Father, for eternal life. Thank you that what I am living in now is temporary, so help me to not focus on any temporary troubles or worries. Father, help me to fix my gaze on what cannot be seen, for the things I see now will soon be gone, but the things we cannot see will last forever. I thank you because you are greater than any troubles I face. I thank you because I am your child and you love me. You carry me through every season of life and you lift my Spirit daily. You protect me from harm and you refresh my soul in you, Jesus. Help me to fix my eyes on you, without being distracted from the daily pressures of this world. In Jesus name I pray, Amen.

Things to consider:

What areas in your life/business are troubling you at the moment? Hand them over to God, knowing that they will be resolved. What choices can you make that will help you fix your eyes on Jesus?

Just like any camera, what you focus on, you develop.

How are you fixing your eyes on Jesus, who is eternal, compared to all of the noise that surrounds us, as you do business with the King?

WEEK 1, DAY 5

Courage

**Begin by taking a moment to stay still in God's presence.
Holy Spirit come, I turn my attention to you.**

Scripture Reading:

Matthew 3:1-10

"In those days John the Baptist came, preaching in the wilderness of Judea and saying, "Repent, for the kingdom of heaven has come near." This is he who was spoken of through the prophet Isaiah:
"A voice of one calling in the wilderness,
'Prepare the way for the Lord, make straight paths for him.'"

John's clothes were made of camel's hair and he had a leather belt around his waist. His food was locusts and wild honey. People went out to him from Jerusalem and all Judea and the whole region of the Jordan. Confessing their sins, they were baptised by him in the Jordan River. But when he saw many of the Pharisees and Sadducees coming to where he was baptising, he said to them: "You brood of vipers! Who warned you to flee from the coming wrath? Produce fruit in keeping with repentance. And do not think you can say to yourselves, 'We have Abraham as our father.' I tell you that out of these stones God can raise up children for Abraham. The ax is already at the root of the trees, and every tree that does not produce good fruit will be cut down and thrown into the fire."

Matthew 14:27

"Jesus immediately said to them: "Take courage! It is I. Don't be afraid."

Devotional Thought:

John the Baptist is a great example of a man full of courage, with a unique ministry of his own. He paved the way for Jesus by calling people to live what they believe and to repent of their sins. John's courageous ministry demonstrated that he had a clear message (vs.1-3): that the most important thing to him was his ministry, not his image (vs. 4-6), and that his conviction was stronger than those who were there to criticise him.

So the question is, what helped John become more courageous? John had a deliberate mission with a straight message. He had a direct motive and a different manner of approaching people. He had strong principles and he had a strong discerning spirit, where he knew who was for him and who was against him.

Devotional Prayer:

Thank you Jesus for you are, always there. You give me the courage to walk on water with you through all of my weaknesses, to know your power and to indulge in your presence. You give me the choice to be humble and have proved yourself in my life by showing me your power and grace. When I doubt and look at the greatness that is opposing me (just like Peter did when he walked on water), I begin to fall. But you, O Lord, are so faithful. You stretch out your arm to me again and again and you rescue me. Thank you Father because you are there for me. In every stormy day, you are my ever-present help when I am doubtful, fearful and lacking faith. Even though, time and time again, I see your miraculous hand in my life, I still doubt. Give me courage, help me to understand and know that you are beside me and with me in every moment of my day. In Jesus mighty name I pray, Amen.

Things to consider:

What giant are you facing today that you need courage for? What action can you take to remind yourself that Jesus is with you in this storm every time you reach this point? What qualities from John the Baptist's ministry do you need to help you in your ministry/workplace?

....

....

....

....

WEEK 2, DAY 1

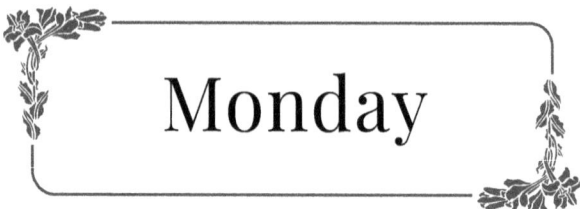

Monday

Essential qualities in Leadership.

**Begin by taking a moment to stay still in God's presence.
Holy Spirit come, I turn my attention to you.**

Scripture Reading:

Acts 6:3-4

"Brothers and sisters, choose seven men from among you who are known to be full of the Spirit and wisdom. We will turn this responsibility over to them and will give our attention to prayer and the ministry of the word."

Devotional thought:

Leaders and workers are always required within the workplace. A good leader actively responds to selecting the right person for the position. In the early church, it was required from them to choose someone with specific qualifications that were from their sphere of influence, to choose someone who was trusted and filled with the Spirit. To choose someone who was competent, wise and responsible.

Devotional prayer:

Father, thank you for your always abundant presence. Thank you for always being by my side. Grant me a continual readiness and devotion to prayer. Open up my eyes and my heart to understand the great privilege you have given me in allowing me free access into your throne room. Give me a heart that is hungry to spend time with you. And as I do, prepare my mind and heart for the work you have for me to build up your Kingdom here on earth. Help me to discern things in the spiritual realm as I embark on choosing leaders and staff in my workplace. Thank you for giving me your wisdom, knowledge and understanding. In Jesus mighty name I pray, Amen.

Things to consider:

On what basis and values do you choose your leaders and staff? Do you need to alter this to incorporate some of the ways the Spirit lead the early Church in choosing critical leaders?

What is God talking to you about today as you spend time in His presence?

WEEK 2, DAY 2

Tuesday

Forever Nourished and Strengthened.

**Begin by taking a moment to stay
still in God's presence.
Holy Spirit come, I turn my attention to you.**

Scripture Readings:

Jeremiah 17:7-8

"But blessed is the man who trusts in the Lord, whose confidence is in him. He will be like a tree planted by the water that sends out its roots by the stream. It does not fear when heat comes; its leaves are always green. It has no worries in a year of drought and never fails to bear fruit."

Devotional thought:

Successful leaders depend on the wisdom of God, not their own. Being planted by the water, where your roots touch the stream is a metaphor describing:

1. Signs of stability in the word
2. Inward nourishment and refreshment from the word
3. Fruitfulness and productivity
4. Strength and durability
5. When in a crisis season, you never experience famine, but you excel
6. Success is your portion

Devotional Prayer:

Thank you, Father, for your Holy Spirit that lives within me. Today, I choose to trust you and put all of my confidence in you. I choose to be planted today by rivers of water that allow for my roots to be nourished through your word. I have no fear because you are my source of strength and nutrition. I am an overcomer because I have your DNA. You provide for me even through times of drought and famine. You call me blessed because I am yours and you are mine. I love you Lord. In Jesus mighty name I pray, Amen.

Things to consider:

Is there a dry place in your world at the moment that you need refreshment, restoration and courage to deal with? This can be your marriage, finances, children, and so on. Please write them below and hand them over to God today.

WEEK 2, DAY 3

Wednesday

No shame or disgrace.

**Begin by taking a moment to stay
still in God's presence.
Holy Spirit come, I turn my attention to you.**

Scripture reading:

Isaiah 45:17

"But Israel shall be saved by the Lord with an everlasting salvation; you shall not be ashamed or disgraced forever and ever."

Devotional thought:

The Lord protects His people and never lets them down. The characteristics of a trusted Christian leader comprise of the following:

1. Have Integrity - their life matches their words.
2. Are Just in the way they do life and don't agree to dishonest profits.
3. Are Convicted - they are not bribed by anything/anyone, no matter the gain.
4. Have a Positive Focus and refuse to dwell on damaging issues.
5. Are Pure - they discipline themselves to stay clean and pure.
6. Are Secure - their identity is firm and stable and are a source of strength to others.

Devotional Prayer:

Father, I thank you that I have been grafted into your covenant with Abraham, so I claim all of your covenant promises and privileges that you have promised Israel. I acknowledge that I need help in my daily life and I know that my help comes from you alone. Save and deliver me from (tell the Lord a certain circumstance that is currently disturbing your peace). Father, bring me to permanent deliverance and salvation out of this circumstance. You promise me in this scripture that I will not be ashamed or disgraced, forever and ever. I wait on you, Lord. Protect me from any kind of shame and disgrace that is trying to put me down. I pray this in your name Jesus, Amen.

Things to consider:

What characteristic do you feel you can improve on to be the best leader God has called you to be?

WEEK 2, DAY 4

My Defender.

**Begin by taking a moment to stay
still in God's presence.
Holy Spirit come, I turn my attention to you.**

Scripture Readings:

Isaiah 54:17

"No weapon formed against you shall prosper, and every tongue which rises against you in judgement you shall condemn. This is the heritage of the servants of the Lord, and their righteousness is from Me,' says the Lord."

Isaiah 55:10-12

"As the rain and the snow come down from heaven, and do not return to it without watering the earth and making it bud and flourish, so that it yields seed for the sower and bread for the eater, so is my word that goes out from my mouth: It will not return to me empty, but will accomplish what I desire and achieve the purpose for which I sent it. You will go out in joy and be led forth in peace; the mountains and hills will burst into song before you, and all the trees of the field will clap their hands."

Devotional Thought:

A victorious leader is found through the participation of a right relationship with God. This is God's promise to you. God will accomplish the goals you have set through spending time in His Word. God's Word bears fruit and God evaluates good communication through His Word. His Word will help bring forth Good results; His Word will help meet your needs; His Word will help perform His will in every situation.

Devotional Prayer:

Thank you, Father, for you promised that all things work for good for those who love you and are called according to your purpose. Father, I see weapons formed against me, but I know that you see them before I do. Thank you that nothing is hidden from your sight and that I am hidden in the secret place of the Most High God, where I am safe. Father, you promised that no weapon formed against me would prosper. Therefore, I ask you to defend me against the enemy's onslaught and totally obliterate the attack against my life. Lord, you said that when the enemy comes in like a flood, the Holy Spirit will raise up a battle standard against him. Father God, I ask you to lift up your battle standard against the enemy and don't allow the enemy to pass through your protection that is around me. Help me to walk with integrity and uprightness, no matter what. Thank you, Lord, that every tongue that rises against me in judgment, you shall condemn. I ask you to fight against every accusation coming from the accuser - Satan himself. Expose every lie that comes against me as the lie that it is. Make the truth plainly known to all parties involved. Make my right standing with you obvious to all people because you said that I am the righteousness of God in Christ. Vindicate me father. In Jesus name I pray, Amen.

Things to Consider:

As a leader, can you evaluate your communication? What fruit does your communication bring?

What are the battles you are facing in this season of your life that you need God to defend you on?

....
....
....
....
....
....
....
....
....

WEEK 2, DAY 5

Friday

You are an Anointed leader.

**Begin by taking a moment to stay
still in God's presence.
Holy Spirit come, I turn my attention to you.**

Scripture readings:

Isaiah 61:1-3

"The Spirit of the Sovereign Lord is on me, because the Lord has anointed me to proclaim good news to the poor. He has sent me to bind up the brokenhearted, to proclaim freedom for the captives and release from darkness for the prisoners, to proclaim the year of the Lord's favour and the day of vengeance of our God, to comfort all who mourn, and provide for those who grieve in Zion— to bestow on them a crown of beauty instead of ashes, the oil of joy instead of mourning, and a garment of praise instead of a spirit of despair. They will be called oaks of righteousness, a planting of the Lord for the display of his splendour."

Isaiah 62:8-9

"The Lord has sworn by His right hand and by the arm of His strength: 'Surely I will no longer give your grain as food to your enemies; and the sons of the foreigner shall not drink your new wine, for which you have laboured. But those who have gathered it shall eat it, and praise the Lord; those who have brought it together shall drink it in My holy courts.'"

Devotional Thought:

God has created you to be an anointed leader, but the question is, what is the calling of an anointed leader?

As we see in the book of Isaiah, he describes that God's servant is anointed to preach good news, heal the brokenhearted, proclaim freedom to the captives, to proclaim the Lord's favour, and to comfort those who mourn.

With that being said, leaders are also anointed to speak and perform supernatural tasks in their workplace, including:

- ♛ Enabling men and women to grow in their ministry and God calling
- ♛ To give a perspective of beauty when others have lost that

- ♛ To provide happiness in a season where others are feeling down
- ♛ To give God the glory in every opportunity available to them and not to man

Devotional Prayer:

Father I praise you because you are faithful! You are a God that sees and knows all things. I have gathered grain in, through service, generosity, giving, prayer and intercession over many years. So I claim your promises over my family and my business, and I claim what I have laboured for to be an abundant harvest for me and the generations to come. Father, I ask you to bring in the new wine for which I have laboured for all these years. I ask that the harvest you release over my life would have accumulated interest over the years that have already passed. Father, I pray your protection over my harvest; I pray that you rebuke the devourer for my sake and to bring me more harvest than I've ever dreamed. In Jesus mighty name I pray, Amen.

Things to consider:

This is a personal time of evaluation of your leadership and how you are assisting others to grow in their gifts and talents. You are anointed to do the work of the Kingdom and now it's time to see how you are pursuing this in your leadership style.

Below, note down areas in your finances that need grain and pray over them a release.

....

....

WEEK 3, DAY 1

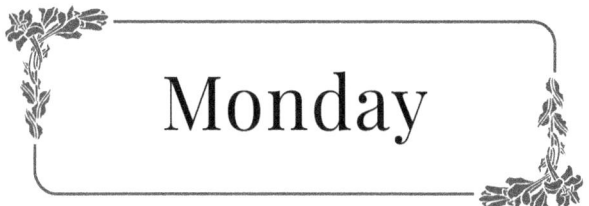

Monday

His Grace is what I need today.

**Begin by taking a moment to stay
still in God's presence.
Holy Spirit come, I turn my attention to you.**

Scripture Readings:

2 Corinthians 12:9

"And He said to me, 'My grace is sufficient for you, for My strength is made perfect in weakness.' Therefore most gladly I will rather boast in my infirmities, that the power of Christ may rest upon me."

Devotional Thought:

In 2 Corinthians chapter 12, Paul links a beautiful vision with a thorn in his flesh. He spoke about how God motivated him through this vision of heaven, yet also how God kept him humble through an opposition - the thorn in the flesh.

Visions for the leader helps them become more passionate about what they do. On the other hand, thorns keep the leader authentic.

Paul understood this very well. The weaker we are as humans, the stronger God becomes within us. Less of us means more of Him, and only a wise leader would understand this.

It is important to understand that:

1. opposition is not from God
2. seeking God for answers to our problems
3. grace is God's answer to our imperfections
4. the bigger the problem, the greater the grace

Devotional prayer:

Father, thank you for your grace of which I have been saved. Thank you for the free gift of salvation that cost Jesus everything, which I received freely. Thank you for your active grace in my life that helps me each and every day, even when I don't notice it.

Your word says that your grace is sufficient for me, because your strength is made perfect in my weakness.

Father, I place before you (tell Father God about the situation you need help - without self-pity).

Father, I confess that I am weak in my own strength, and without you I can do nothing. Your word doesn't day "My grace plus your work are sufficient". It says, "My grace is sufficient." So Father, I thank you because your grace is able to meet the totality of all of my needs, all by itself, without me doing anything. Without you Jesus, I am inadequate, but I am totally complete in Christ Jesus, and I thank you for that.

Pour out your grace upon my life. Let your grace be the driving force that propels everything in my life. Make your grace tangible in my life - as a tangible assistance, tangible guidance and a tangible help.

I ask you Father, by your grace and power, to do what I could never do by my own work. I ask you to perform miracles that only can be done by you and your grace - things beyond what I could ever strive or labour for.

Manifest miracles in my life and business through the driving force of your grace. Help me to notice how you answer my prayers, to praise you and give you all the glory in my life. In Jesus mighty name I pray, Amen.

Things to consider:

Is there something in your world at the moment that is a thorn? How is God speaking to you through this situation as a motivation to have more of Him, and less of you?

Below, write down the situation you need God's miraculous hand of help in.

....
....

WEEK 3, DAY 2

Angelic Protection.

**Begin by taking a moment to stay
still in God's presence.
Holy Spirit come, I turn my attention to you.**

Scripture Readings:

Psalm 91:11-12

"For He shall give His angels charge over you, to keep you in all your ways. In their hands they shall bear you up, lest you dash you foot against the stone."

Devotional thought:

Psalm 91 is one of the most comforting Psalms in the bible. It is full of security measures for the believer to enjoy through their strong faith in God. As a leader and business operator, you too can benefit from these amazing promises.

1. Verse 1 & 2 describe the presence of God showing leaders that you don't have to do life alone and that God is with you today.
2. Verses 3 & 4 show the amazing protection of God over you as a leader when you take risks and He keeps you safe as you do that.
3. The peace of God is available to you (Vs. 5-6) so you don't have to feel insecure as you step into the unknown. Start positioning yourself for that Angelic peace by fully surrendering.
4. God sees things from a completely different perspective from us (Vs. 7-10). He keeps us secure with an eternal view of life.
5. The provision of God (Vs. 11-13) for your business and your world are given to you regardless of your needs. He always meets your needs.
6. The power of God is evident in your life (Vs. 14-16) as He helps you achieve your goals and delivers you from any challenge or adversity that is facing you in this season.

Devotional Prayer:

Father God, I thank you for the opportunity to be able to dwell in the secret place of the Most High - the secret place of your presence, continually. Help me to abide under your shadow. I believe that you are my refuge and fortress; you are my God, in whom I trust. Thank you, father God, for sending your angels to take charge over me and keep me in all of your ways.

So many times in your Word, you show me examples of the angels helping your people whenever they needed it. Like when:

- ♛ *the angel brought food to Elijah in the wilderness*
- ♛ *when the angel released Peter from prison*
- ♛ *when the angels rescued Lot and his family before Sodom was destroyed*
- ♛ *when the angel brought an encouraging message to Joseph when he found out Mary was pregnant*
- ♛ *when the angel ministered to Jesus in Gethsemane, and*
- ♛ *when an angel showed the apostle John all around heaven.*

I thank you, Lord, that your angels are also at work in my life. Lord, in the same way you rescued Peter from prison, I ask that you send your angels to rescue me in that same way.

I ask you Lord to give me triple the amount of angelic assistance I currently am receiving in my life.

Father, I ask you to send your angels to carry direct messages from you to me. Send your angels to show me Heaven and heavenly things. Send them to protect, minister and strengthen me. I ask that you send the angels to do warfare on my behalf and bring me provision and resources from Heaven.

Father, I ask you to help me today to test the spirits when I encounter them so that I know that they are holy angels sent by you.

Help me see your angels, just in the same way people in the Bible interacted with the angels. Thank you, Father, for your faithfulness and the way you answer my prayers. In Jesus mighty name I pray, Amen.

Things to consider:

What is the most comforting verse you find in Psalm 91? Which promise do you need to hold on more to in this season?

List things below that you can surrender today so that you can position yourself for God's angelic presence.

WEEK 3, DAY 3

The Author of Peace and Order.

**Begin by taking a moment to stay
still in God's presence.
Holy Spirit come, I turn my attention to you.**

Scripture Reading:

1 Corinthians 14:33

"For God is not the author of confusion but of peace, as in all the churches of the saints."

Also in your own time read that full chapter… 1 Corinthians 14:1-40

Devotional thought:

Leaders are generally very organised people. Paul wrote to the Corinthian church in a time where there was chaos and he wanted to bring order to the church. Paul urged the Corinthian church to do everything in a fitting and orderly way, as the Corinthian Church were abusing their gifts and calling. They were instead trying to bring attention to themselves. This teaches us Kingdom business owners/leaders a few things about organisation:

1. Identify and go after your top priorities
2. Aim to put into practice what will benefit most people in the workplace
3. Clearly communicate what is required from your team
4. View things from a different perspective
5. Make sure everything is done in an appropriate manner

Devotional Prayer:

Thank you, Father, for you are a God of order and want things done in excellence, because you are the God of excellence. I thank you because you are a God of peace, not confusion. I submit to your Lordship in this area of my life. Since Peace is who you are, I acknowledge you Lord over my life, and I ask you to manifest peace in every area of my life.

I confess that I need your help and peace daily. I ask that you interfere in (say situation(s) you currently facing chaos in). Father, I admit that I cannot straighten these situations out without your help, but I know that I can do all things through Christ who gives me strength. Father, I believe that you are the author of peace.

> *Help me by going before me to make every crooked path straight so that your Kingdom can come and your will be done.*
>
> *I ask that you help me initiate peace in my life and help me to also seek peace and pursue it. Initiate order in my life, Jesus. Bring order from every chaos that is surrounding me. I speak into every situation in my life and command them to realign themselves and manifest order, instead of chaos. I ask you to show me what to do, and help me actually do it, to create peace in every area of my life. Anoint me to be an organised person. Help me get my environment clean (my house, office, studio…). I ask you to order my steps in your Word. Help me to make my paths straight, and come into my life and display your glory, Lord Jesus. Help me notice your answers to my prayers. I thank you for you create order from chaos. In Jesus mighty name I pray, Amen.*

Things to consider:

Which areas of your life do you need God to interfere into with peace? Is there an area in your life that you identify with that you need God to bring order to?

....
....
....
....
....
....
....

WEEK 3, DAY 4

Thursday

A Thousand-Fold blessing.

Begin by taking a moment to stay still in God's presence. Holy Spirit come, I turn my attention to you.

Scripture Readings:

Deuteronomy 1:11

"May the Lord God of your fathers make you a thousand times more numerous than you are, and bless you as He has promised you!"

Devotional thought:

Deuteronomy is a great book in the Bible that is full of leadership. Moses retells and reminds his people the hand of God and the way God chose

His leaders. Through Moses and his life, God displays powerful leadership, perspective, vision, purpose and principles to guide the Israelites. A Prophetic declaration is spoken over the people as leaders are appointed.

1. In Deuteronomy 1:6-8, God prepares his children to see the land that He had promised them.
2. Then God teaches them to share the load through delegation (Deuteronomy 1:9-14).
3. Leaders were then appointed (Deuteronomy 1:15).
4. Then a structure in the leadership team was put into place (Deuteronomy 1:16-18).

Devotional Prayer:

Thank you, Father God, for how far you have brought me. You took me from the land of my enemies and now I am much closer to the crossing over into the Promised Land. My enemies stood between me and the Promised Land, trying to prevent me from receiving my blessing. Thank you for being with me and going with me every step of the way.

(Remind God of every promise He has promised you - don't leave any promises out). Your promises are Yes and Amen when they are in your will, so I thank you in advance for granting me these promises. Father, I ask you to pull good things that were originally intended for my future into the present time. Give me a thousand-fold increase of every good thing you have already done for me. I ask that you help me notice your answers to my prayers and I thank you for the thousand-fold increase. Thank you, for you are so faithful. Thank you for blessing me as you promised you will. In Jesus mighty name I pray, Amen.

Things to consider:

Write down the declarations spoken over you and what God has promised you over the years that you are expecting to see Him fulfil.

How does the way God displays his powerful leadership through Moses differ to the way you lead now?

WEEK 3, DAY 5

Friday

The Lord will fight for me today.

**Begin by taking a moment to stay
still in God's presence.
Holy Spirit come, I turn my attention to you.**

Scripture reading:

Exodus 14:13-14

"And Moses said to the people, 'Do not be afraid. Stand still and see the salvation of the Lord, which He will accomplish for you today. For the Egyptians whom you see today, you shall see again no more forever. The Lord will fight for you, and you shall hold your peace.'"

Also read all of Exodus Chapter 14 in your own time.

Devotional Thought:

Exodus 14 shows how the Egyptian army put pressure on the Israelites, causing Moses had to show them how he would react in a crisis. But because Moses had seen the power and hand of God in action before in his life, Moses wasn't disturbed. He had ultimate peace. So Moses gained credibility in this situation as the Lord fought for him before their very own eyes.

What gave Moses the credibility before the people was the fact that he was calm, not anxious, about the situation (Ex 14:13). He showed confidence and wasn't worried (Ex 14:13), he spoke clarity to the people and didn't cause confusion (Ex 14:15), and he forecasted a great vision instead of showing he was confused (Ex 14:21-22).

Devotional Prayer:

Father God, I thank you because you are my Rock, my Shield, my Defence and my Strong Tower. I thank you that I am hidden in the secret place of the Most High, where I am safe from all harm and danger. Father God, I ask you to continue to fill me with your perfect love and make me perfect in love so that I will never be afraid. Your Word says that perfect love casts out the spirit of fear and delivers me from fear. Father God, I choose to rest in you today. I ask you to help me rest as well, since I can do nothing without you, but I can do all things, including rest, through Christ who gives me strength. I ask you to do all the fighting for me in my situation(s). Help me to stand still. Help me to put and keep my Spiritual armour on at all times. I ask you, Father God, to work your salvation for me in all situations. I ask you, Papa, to bring me total and complete victory while I stand still and hold my peace. Bring me such a radical victory that I never see my enemies or this battle ever again after this battle. I ask you to help me see you and the armies of angels that will work and fight on my behalf.

Father God, I declare that you would make me credible in front of each person that you have placed in my path through victorious and Supernatural results. I pray that people will see these good and victorious results and glorify you in Heaven. Thank you for your powerful hand in my life. You have shown me that I am victorious through you. Show me your glory again and again in every situation that I face. I believe that you are my defender and that I am victorious in you.

Thank you Father.

In Jesus mighty name I pray, Amen.

Things to consider:

In what area do you need God to fight for you today?

In what circumstances have you previously seen the hand of God in your life that encourage you to continue to move forward?

Consider learning from Moses' leadership style how to react in a crisis. How can you improve the way you lead to gain credibility before your team, just like Moses did?

....
....
....
....
....
....

WEEK 4, DAY 1

 # Monday

Servant Leadership.

**Begin by taking a moment to stay
still in God's presence.
Holy Spirit come, I turn my attention to you.**

Scripture readings:

Isaiah 50:7

"For the Lord God will help Me; therefore I will not be disgraced; therefore I have set My face like a flint, and I know that I will not be ashamed."

Also read Isaiah 52:12 and 13.

Devotional thought:

The best model of servant leadership shown in all of History is Jesus Christ through the way he modelled sacrifice. He gave up the best of Heaven to fulfil such a beautiful role here on earth.

Isaiah 53 describes a beautiful exchange: the sacrifice that Jesus did. He took our pain, suffering, failures and sin so that we could have his healing, success, righteousness and victory. While this amazing package is available to everyone, leaders have a unique way of gaining benefit from this sacrifice.

1. His sacrifice took care of our insecurities, infirmities and brokenness, and through that, we have gained stable emotions and security.
2. His sacrifice took care of our sins and short-comings, and through that, we have gained forgiveness from guilt and shame.
3. His sacrifice took care of our diseases and sickness, and through that, we have gained healing and wholeness.
4. His sacrifice took care of our mental confusions and pain, and through that, we gain Peace of mind.
5. His sacrifice took care of our weaknesses and through that, we have gained His supernatural strength.

Devotional Prayer:

Thank you, Father God, for sending your one and only son, Jesus, to be my example and teach me how to live. The flint is used in this verse figuratively to describe perseverance. Thank you for setting His face like a flint to carry out the Father's will. Thank you, Jesus, for setting your face like a flint to go to the Cross. Even though it was hard, you did not quit on us. You didn't stop. You did what the Father told you to do. Thank you for the ultimate sacrifice that you took upon yourself for me. Thank you for being that perfect example of carrying out the Father's will. Help me to be the same. If I ever felt like quitting, or if I did actually quit, Father, I repent and confess my disobedience to your will for my life. I ask you to fill me with your Spirit to be more and more like you, Father. I choose to submit my will to you and your Lordship to become the perfect example in my life. I draw a line in the sand today and I ask you to do surgery on me and take out the "quit" in me right now. I ask you to work in my heart and for the Holy Spirit to bear the fruit of patience, faithfulness and long suffering in me. Father, from this day forward, I want there to be no more quit in me at all. I choose to set my face like a flint to obey you, just like Jesus did, no matter what. I ask you to work in me to do your good will. Help me and keep me from being disgraced or ashamed. I thank you, for you are a God who answers prays. In Jesus mighty name I pray, Amen.

Things to consider:

What positive action will you take to help you never quit (or even think of quitting) again?

What can I learn from Jesus' example of servant leadership?

What painful situations can you exchange today for what Jesus has sacrificed for you. remembering that the price has been paid in full?

....

....

WEEK 4, DAY 2

Tuesday

No more affliction.

**Begin by taking a moment to stay
still in God's presence.
Holy Spirit come, I turn my attention to you.**

Scripture Reading:

Nahum 1:12-13

"Thus says the Lord:
'Though they are safe, and likewise many, yet in this manner they will be cut down when he passes through. Though I have afflicted you, I will afflict you no more; for now I will break off his yoke from you, and burst your bonds apart.'"

Devotional thought:

In the book of Nahum, we see God leading through two different positions: as a Judge and as a Father. Through that, God confronts and He also disciplines. God modelled for leaders everywhere how to deal with situations as a Judge, and on the other hand, how to deal with them as a Father. Although they both demonstrate a beautiful balance between the two, below are the ways that God teaches us the balance of leadership through being a Judge and a Father:

1. As a Judge, God was envious for His people (1:2) and as a Father, God the leader, was slow to anger (1:3).
2. As a Judge, God was a conqueror (1:2) and as a Father, God leads us through His goodness (1:7).
3. As a Judge, God was angry (1:2) and as a Father, God is a fortress (1:7).
4. As a Judge, God is all powerful (1:3) and as a Father, God is a resting place (1:7).
5. As a Judge, God punishes those in the wrong (1:3) and as a Father, God gives freedom (1:13).

Devotional Prayer:

Father God, I love you so much! Thank you for always fighting on my side. Thank you for refining me and purifying me. I acknowledge that you know best. I acknowledge you as my Lord and ask you to purify me continually to conform to you to be the image of Christ. I acknowledge that I wrestle not against flesh and blood, but against the enemy's forces of darkness. So, even in the situations in which I need breakthrough, my enemies are not people, but are rather those same forces of darkness. Thank you Lord that Jesus already overcame every power of the wicked one and rendered him ineffective through Jesus' life, death and resurrection. I plead the blood of Jesus over my situation. I ask you, Father God, to cover every aspect of my situation (name every situation) with Jesus' blood. I ask you Father to bring forth your perfect will in these situations - the perfect peace and victory that Jesus died and shed His blood to obtain. Thank you Father God for fighting for me again. I ask you to obliterate the attack and forces of the enemy off every part of my life, in Jesus' name. I ask you to break the enemy's yoke and influence off me. I ask you, Father God, to burst apart every chain and bond that is holding me, right now, today. Father, I pray all these things now, today, for that is what Nahum 1:12-13 says He will do! Thank you, Papa God, that there will be no more affliction in my life! Thank you for not allowing me to be afflicted anymore. I ask you to bring me and everything about me into perfect peace and shalom—a state of total wholeness and unity with you, Lord, and your will, inside and out, with nothing missing and nothing broken. I thank you Father for all these things in Jesus mighty name I pray, Amen.

Things to consider:

List below the situations you are believing God to break you free from.

How can I learn from God's example in Nahum, the balance of being a Judge and a Father in every leadership situation that I am faced with?

....

....

....

....

WEEK 4, DAY 3

Wednesday

Establish the Work of Our Hands - Time Management.

**Begin by taking a moment to stay still in God's presence.
Holy Spirit come, I turn my attention to you.**

Scripture readings:

Psalm 90:12-17

"Teach us to number our days, that we may gain a heart of wisdom. Return, O Lord! How long? And have compassion on Your servants. Oh, satisfy us early with Your mercy, that we may rejoice and be glad all our days! Make us glad according to the days in which You have afflicted us, the years in which we have seen evil.

Let Your work appear to Your servants, and Your glory to their children. And let the beauty of the Lord our God be upon us, and establish the work of our hands for us; yes, establish the work of our hands."

Devotional thought:

Psalm 90 is a prayer Moses prayed as he had seen his people wander for 40 years in the wilderness. We see through this passage of scripture the importance of time management for leaders. If leaders have a strong sense of time management, they will be able to achieve something significant, and have a great sense of satisfaction in doing so, which will motivate them to do even more. Leaders are not time wasters; they use there time wisely.

Devotional Prayer:

Father God, I trust you with all of my heart, but my circumstances have been out of alignment with your Word long enough. I am reminding You of what You promised. I am reminding You of the exact Scriptures in which You promised those things, too. Father God, you are merciful and gracious, slow to anger and abounding in mercy and loving kindness. You are compassionate and your compassion always moves you to do something. Papa God, pour out your compassion and mercy on me. Manifest your compassion and mercy in my specific situation (point out that you know who He is and what He is like, so you have every right to ask Him to do and be those things in your life and situation right now).
I ask you to fill me with peace, joy and power. Help me be right with you and obedient to you in every area of my life. I ask you, Father God, specifically to bring me reward, harvest, good fruit/results and joy right now in the same proportion, or greater, as all the hard days that I have previously gone through. I ask you to

manifest Your might and power in my life; that Your mighty hand and outstretched arm would work on my behalf, both in ways I expect and in ways I haven't thought to ask. I ask you to manifest Your glory to me and my children. I ask you to give me and my descendants a magnificent obsession with Jesus, the Son of God. I ask you, Papa, to mark me with your beauty, power, anointing, aroma and glory. I ask you to make these things actually visible on my face and in every part of my life. I ask you to establish the work of my hands. I ask you to bless all the good work I have done and bring me a harvest. I ask you to cover any bad works that I have done with Jesus' blood. Forgive me and spare me from receiving bad fruit from those things. I ask you for double blessing, double favour, and double results from every good work or labor I have sown, ever, in my whole life. Thank you for all these things Father. In Jesus mighty name I pray, Amen.

Things to consider:

List below what you are currently sowing time into that you want to see harvest produced in.

What habits can you put in place that will prevent you from being a time waster so that you can achieve accelerated results in all that you place your hands to?

....
....
....
....
....
....

WEEK 4, DAY 4

Thursday

Arise and Shine

**Begin by taking a moment to stay still in God's presence.
Holy Spirit come, I turn my attention to you.**

Scripture readings:

Isaiah 60:1

"Arise, shine; for your light has come! And the glory of the Lord is risen upon you."

Devotional thought:

As Kingdom leaders, it is difficult to live a life that is passive. Kingdom leaders posses a passion and motivation from within them. As leaders, we shouldn't compromise walking out our calling with the pressures that we face in the world and the things that drain us emotionally, spiritually and physically. It's not enough for the leader to just "arise"; the leader must also "shine" their skills, talents and God given gifts into the world. The rest of that scripture also assures you that the Glory of the Lord is upon you as you arise and shine in your workplace.

Devotional Prayer:

Father God, I love You and I want to obey Your every command and every word. I acknowledge out loud that I see your command to arise and shine. I acknowledge and accept that this command is for me. Father, I choose to arise and shine now. Your promise in Psalm 32:8 says that you will instruct me and teach me in the way I should go and you will guide me with your eyes upon me. I ask you, Father, to lead me today in the steps that you want me to take. I repent of the days I've done my own things and gone my own way, but today, Father, I ask you to guide me with your Word, which is a lamp to my feet and a light to my path. I as you to help me obey you by taking the small steps I need to take. I ask you to help me step out in faith, even if it's just to put my toes into something to see if it turns out to be your will. Father God, I ask for your wisdom, understanding and increased Spiritual discernment over my life. I ask you to part the waters for me as soon as I step into the things that are in your will. I ask you to deliver me from your permissive will and keep me in your perfect will instead. Thank you, Father God, for your glory that has arisen upon me. Thank you that your light has come. Thank you that I will have success this time around, for "your light has come"!

Thank you for considering me to be precious enough to make me a home for your glory! I ask you to glorify your own name over and over in my life! I thank you for all these things in the mighty name of Jesus, Amen.

Things to consider:

Write down below steps that you need to take to arise and shine in purpose and passion for the things of God.

Highlight the pressures of the world that drain you emotionally, Spiritually and Physically.

And what are the ways that you will take to prevent them from getting in the way of your passion and motivation?

....
....
....
....
....
....
....
....
....
....
....

WEEK 4, DAY 5

Friday

The Wealth of the Roar Shall Be Turned to Me

**Begin by taking a moment to stay still in God's presence.
Holy Spirit come, I turn my attention to you.**

Scripture readings:

Isaiah 60:3-5

"The Gentiles shall come to your light and kings to the brightness of your rising. "Lift up your eyes all around, and see: they all gather together, they come to you; your sons shall come from afar, and your daughters shall be nursed at your side.

Then you shall see and become radiant, and your heart shall swell with joy; because the abundance of the sea shall be turned to you, the wealth of the Gentiles shall come to you."

Devotional thought:

What are the characteristics of a leader? Most leaders don't have a desire to be amazing leaders. Rather, they desire to be amazing people. Leadership qualifications are all about the personal attributes and qualifications of the individual. Naturally, when a leader does life well, followers are attracted to their lifestyle.

There are four very significant elements in the life of the leader that we must pay attention to in order to be successful:

1. Character contributes to doing the right thing, even when circumstances are difficult.
2. Courage contributes towards stepping out and taking risks to achieve your vision.
3. Perspective contributes to the way you view situations to reach your goal.
4. Favour contributes towards the way you empower others and attract them to follow your conviction.

Devotional Prayer:

Thank you, Father, for calling me to arise and shine. Thank you that your glory is sitting upon me and can actually be seen on my face. I ask you to give me huge influence for your name's sake—but only as much influence as I can steward well for you, and no influence at all that I would use for evil. I ask you, Lord, to bring people to me from all over the world who will see you through me. I ask you to send me people of influence that I can impact for your glory. I ask you to bring your sons and daughters to me from the four corners of the earth. I ask you to show me your answers to my prayers, fulfil me, and overwhelm my heart with joy and radiance. I ask you, Father, to bring me financial wealth as well—the wealth of your roar over me, I declare! I insist that, according to your Word, the wealth of the roar would be turned to me right now! I ask you, Jesus, the Lion of Judah, to roar over my finances today! I ask you to provide for me abundantly, according to your riches in glory in Christ Jesus! I ask you to send me the wealth of the Gentiles. Father God, I remind you that you said the blessing of the Lord makes rich, and you add no sorrow to it. I ask you to bless me with your blessings that make me rich and that I will carry no sorrow with them. I ask you to help me notice and thank you for every single thing you do for me! I thank you in advance for the blessing that is coming my way. In Jesus mighty name I pray, Amen.

Things to consider:

What blessing are you believing for today?

Are you a leader that desires to lead well? Or are you a leader that just wants to be admired by others?

What element from the qualifications of the leader do you believe that you need to work on more in your life?

....

....

WEEK 5, DAY 1

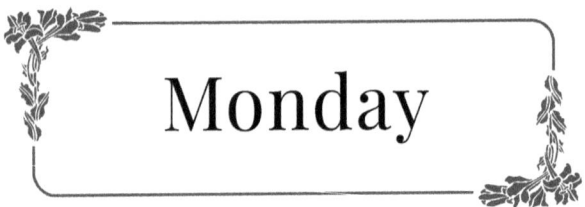

Monday

Do Not Be Weary In Doing Well!

**Begin by taking a moment to stay
still in God's presence.
Holy Spirit come, I turn my attention to you.**

Scripture Reading

Galatians 6:9

"And let us not be weary in well doing: for in due season we shall reap, if we faint not."

Devotional Thought:

As we have been praying for 20 days now, you may be feeling discouraged if you haven't seen breakthrough in your circumstances yet. If that is the case, and this is you, Father God wants you to know that you are plowing right now. You are plowing up the breakthrough. Search for little answers to prayer that have happened and are happening over the next few days. But the answers to your prayers are about to burst open in the heavenlies.

I would encourage you to go and read Daniel Chapter 10 now. Reading it will build your faith in this season. In that chapter, Daniel sets his face to the Lord for three weeks (21 days). When the answer came, the heavenly messenger was sent to Daniel and said that he had been dispatched from heaven, when Daniel first began to pray. However, there was a battle in the heavenlies for three weeks that delayed his answer.

The Lord wants you to know that there is a battle in the heavenlies for your answer too. But do not fear: God is fighting the battle to get your breakthrough through the resistance and into your lap. You already asked Him to fight for you, remember?

So keep contending! Keep plowing! Keep it up and heap up those prayers at the feet of Father God! Come boldly in front of the throne of grace, where you may obtain mercy, and find grace to help in time of need! Father God IS listening. He IS answering.

If you have received breakthrough in a specific area or many areas, it's time to write praise points, thanking God for what He has done so far.

Praise points / Prayer Points:

....

WEEK 5, DAY 2

 # Tuesday

The Former Rain and the Latter Rain.

**Begin by taking a moment to stay still in God's presence.
Holy Spirit come, I turn my attention to you.**

Scripture Reading:

Joel 2:23

Be glad then, you children of Zion, and rejoice in the Lord your God; for He has given you the former rain faithfully, and He will cause the rain to come down for you—the former rain, and the latter rain in the first month."

Devotional thought:

Leaders know how to connect with people by being pertinent. How can you relate to the people you lead? Joel uses relevant events of his time to share incredible truth. In the same way, you too can get the attention of your people with a current event to illustrate and prophesy God's powerful truth over them.

Three ways you can do this is by being innovative, constant (continuing to do this), and stable (without contradicting information).

Devotional Prayer:

Father, I thank you for all the mercy drops of answered prayers you have already answered to this date in my life. Thank you for bringing me to where I am and for never leaving me, nor forsaking me. Thank you for helping me seek you during this set-aside time of consecration with breakthrough prayer. Thank you for being so faithful to always provide all my needs. As I read your Word here, and it says that you will continue to pour out as you have already done, I just want to thank you for that. Father, thank you for promising and manifesting more than what I pray for. In my life, your Word promises that you'll continue doing what you've always done, but you'll also add more to it (the former plus the latter rain). I ask you to pour out for me both the former rain—the provision you have always manifest; the mercy drops—PLUS the latter rain—the HUGE provision, manifest promises and answers to prayer that you have promised me. I ask you to pour this out on me right NOW. I ask you to continue pouring it out even after these daily breakthrough prayers. I am reminding you of what you have promised me. Thank you for all of your mercy drops. I know that the mercy drops, though needed and lovely, are not fulfillment of what you said you would do. I ask you, Father, to do the full quota of what you said you would do and do it now. Father, I'm reminded of the scripture in 1 John 5:14-15, which says: "Now this is the confidence that we have in Him, that if we ask anything according to His will, He hears us. And if we know that He hears us, whatever we ask, we know that we have the petitions that we have asked of Him." Thank you for hearing my prayer. Thank you, Holy Spirit, for helping me pray these things. In Jesus mighty name I pray, Amen.

Things to consider:

What are the promises that God has promised you (through prophetic words, dreams or visions) that you would like to see fulfilled?

Think about how relevant you are to the people you are leading and point down below ways you can improve to give glory to God through you.

....
....
....
....
....
....
....
....
....
....

WEEK 5, DAY 3

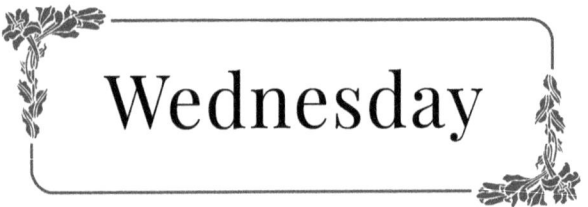

Wednesday

Ask, and You Shall Receive.

**Begin by taking a moment to stay
still in God's presence.
Holy Spirit come, I turn my attention to you.**

Scripture reading:

Matthew 7:7-11

"Ask, and it will be given to you; seek, and you will find; knock, and it will be opened to you. For everyone who asks receives, and he who seeks finds, and to him who knocks it will be opened.
Or what man is there among you who, if his son asks for bread, will give him a stone? Or if he asks for a fish, will he give him a serpent? If you then, being evil, know how to give good gifts to your children, how much

more will your Father who is in heaven give good things to those who ask Him!"

Also read The Beatitudes in Matthew Chapters 5,6 & 7.

Devotional thought:

Did you know that to develop better leadership skills we must begin by adjusting our attitude? The most famous message Jesus preached was the Sermon on the Mount, and this sermon was totally focused on the heart of the people there that were listening. Jesus began by teaching His disciples and then His followers grew to a massive crowd.

As Jesus preached, He demonstrated that the way to develop our leadership skills is to begin by shaping the perspective of our followers.

In The Beatitudes, Jesus shaped and challenged the people's perspective on spiritual depletion and success, sadness and mourning, meekness and gentleness, passion and hunger, mercy and compassion, purity and honesty, peacemaking and vengeance, oppression and adversity.

How are you challenging and shaping the perspective of the people you lead?

Devotional Prayer:

Father, I thank you for everything you have done already and for hearing all my prayers so far. Thank you that your ear is bent toward me and inclined to my cry. I ask you, Holy Spirit, to show me if there is anything I need to get right with you before I go on. (If He shows you something, confess it, repent of it, ask Papa's forgiveness, and ask Him to fill you with His Spirit where that was). Father, I thank you for caring about me so much and for being such a good Father.

Thank you that your Word does not return to you void; it always accomplishes the thing you sent it for when I pray it back to you. Father, this passage says specifically that if I ask, it will be given to me.
(Take a moment and decide on a single thing to ask God for today and ask Him for that thing very specifically and thank Him for giving it to you).

Father, this passage also says that if I seek something I need, I will find it.
(Decide on one thing that you're looking for and ask God to lead you to it. It could be a missing item; an answer or solution to a problem; an open door somewhere; etc. Ask God to help you seek this one thing that you're looking for diligently, since seeking is the pre-requisite to finding in this passage. Thank Him for showing you where the thing is that you need to find).

Father, your Word says that if you knock, doors will be opened to you. (Decide on one opportunity or open door that you need and ask the Father to open that door for you, in agreement with His Word. Ask Him to help you knock on that door, since you have to knock on the door in order to have it opened to you according to this passage. Thank Him for opening that door).

Father, I ask you to give me all the best gifts, the good and perfect gifts that are in agreement with your perfect will. I ask you to give me even more than I've asked for; to help me find even more than I sought for and to open even more doors for me than I've knocked on. In Jesus mighty name I pray, Amen.

Things to consider:

As we read in The Beatitudes and today's devotional thought, Jesus challenged the perspective of His audience.

How are you challenging and shaping the perspective of the people you lead?

What do you need to work on to improve your skills in doing this as a leader?

WEEK 5, DAY 4

Thursday

Receiving the Kingdom

**Begin by taking a moment to stay still in God's presence.
Holy Spirit come, I turn my attention to you.**

Scripture Readings:

Luke 12:29-32

"And do not seek what you should eat or what you should drink, nor have an anxious mind. For all these things the nations of the world seek after, and your Father knows that you need these things.
But seek the Kingdom of God, and all these things shall be added to you. Do not fear, little flock, for it is your Father's good pleasure to give you the kingdom."

Also read all of Luke Chapter 12.

Devotional Thought:

Luke Chapter 12 is filled with many ways to navigate life. But throughout this chapter, Jesus provided many great opportunities to teach His disciples on issues such as integrity, anxiety, convictions, problem solving, greed, jealousy, priorities and trusting God.

Why did Jesus teach His disciples on these topics? This is because Jesus wanted to show them how to live a successful life.

Devotional Prayer:

Father, I thank you because John 4:18 tells me that it's God's perfect love that casts out fear. Because of this, I can conclude that Jesus commanded me not to fear because I have the perfect love of my Father God. In the scripture above, Jesus ties the command not to fear—which is possible only because we have Father's perfect love—to the fact that the Father loves to give us the Kingdom. In other words, Jesus is saying, "Father God loves you, so it makes Him happy to give you everything—the entire Kingdom."

Thank you Jesus for these words of breakthrough.

These words of Jesus are breakthrough words.

John 3:16 says, "For God so loved the world that He gave His only begotten Son ...", and 1 John 3:1 says, "Behold what manner of love the Father has bestowed upon us, that we should be called children of God."

Father, you give because you love. Your giving automatically comes with your love. So the revelation I have is that I am loved by you, Father.

The same way I love to give to my children—just to warm their heart—and the same way I'd never see my children lacking for anything if I can help it—my Father loves to give in the same way.

The difference between me and you, Father God, is that my capacity to give to my children is finite. Some things I can help with, but other things, I cannot.

But Papa God, you never have that problem. Everything in Heaven and earth is yours and all power belongs to you. There is absolutely nothing you can't do, and absolutely nothing you won't do either. You'll give me everything and anything that's good ... just because you love me and you show me that when you say, "Fear not, little flock. It is the Father's good pleasure to give you the Kingdom". So Father, I repent for every time I have focused on and worried about trying to provide my own basic needs, instead of keeping my eyes on Jesus and letting Papa handle it and provide for me. I ask you to forgive me and fill me with your Spirit in those places. I acknowledge that your Kingdom is not meat and drink, but righteousness, peace, joy and power (Romans 14:17; 1 Corinthians 4:20). So I thank you for making me the righteousness of God in Jesus Christ. I ask you, Papa, to fill me with your shalom peace (nothing missing, nothing broken) today. I ask you to fill me with your joy, which is your strength. I ask you to fill me with power by your Spirit, who lives within me. Thank you that the same Spirit who raised Jesus from the dead dwells inside of me. I ask for the Holy Spirit to bear His fruit powerfully in me today. I Ask you Father to re-adjust my priorities to help me seek first your Kingdom—your righteousness, peace, joy and power—and intimacy with you every day, instead of spending unnecessary energy and brain power in the sin of worry. I ask you to help me keep my mind on You, Father, to set my mind and keep it set on things above, where Christ is, seated at the right hand of God. I ask you to help me walk on water as I keep my eyes on you. I ask you to give me every good and perfect gift that you have in mind for me today. I ask you for double blessing in every area, and even more! Thank you Father for giving me *the Kingdom as I seek first Your Kingdom and Your righteousness! In Jesus mighty name, Amen.*

Things to consider:

The Lord's perspective on living a successful life includes some major headings listed above. How can you be successful through these points? Use Luke Chapter 12 to guide you to your answers.

WEEK 5, DAY 5

Friday

Father's Dreams for Your Life.

**Begin by taking a moment to stay
still in God's presence.
Holy Spirit come, I turn my attention to you.**

Scripture Readings:

John 16:12-15

"I still have many things to say to you, but you cannot bear them now. However, when He, the Spirit of truth, has come, He will guide you into all truth; for He will not speak on His own authority, but whatever He hears He will speak; and He will tell you things to come.

He will glorify Me, for He will take of what is Mine and declare it to you. All things that the Father has are Mine. Therefore I said that He will take of Mine and declare it to you."

Also read John 17:11-26

Devotional thought:

At the end of Jesus' life, He was well aware of His inner circle and who He trained to carry the Kingdom. When Jesus prayed, He specifically prayed for their faith, their happiness, their destiny, their faithfulness, their productivity, their friendships and their family.

When Jesus knew He had twelve hours left of His life, He dedicated it all to prayer. Prayer is foundational to the life of every leader. The prayers of a leader that are done in private and behind closed doors are much more important than what is done in public. The people you lead watch what you do, but it's actually what's unseen (prayer) that reveals so much about the leader's commitments and concerns. Prayer will keep the leader dependant on God as he acknowledges His name daily. It will sustain the heart of the leader.

Prayer is a weapon. If you lead people, you must saturate them in prayer.

Devotional Prayer:

Thank you Lord for sending your Holy Spirit to live inside me when I gave my life to Jesus. Give me the credibility to be able to lead the people you have entrusted me with. Thank you for your promise that the Holy Spirit will guide me into all truth. Father, I ask you to give me wisdom and understanding about every situation in my life. I ask you to give me wisdom, understanding and revelation about Spiritual things so that I can see Jesus clearly. I pray for the Holy Spirit to tell me the Father's dreams for my life—those things that are to come. I ask the Lord to change the way in which I operate so that it glorifies your Holy Name. I ask you to change my perspective and teach me how to think like you think. I ask the Holy Spirit to glorify Jesus in my life. I pray that in all that I do in my life for you, Father, gets all of the glory and that I would get none of your glory. I ask you to change my heart if you find anything in me that wants to steal any of your glory. I ask you, Father, for the Holy Spirit to take what belongs to Jesus and declare, show, reveal and transmit all of these things to me. I ask you to speak heavenly things into my life, for your Word creates the thing that is spoken. Father, I ask you to show me more and more about what you have in store for my life. I ask you to help me believe when the Holy Spirit shows me my Father's dreams! I ask you to pour out your Spirit of grace and supplication on me and help me pray into whatever you show me about my Father's dreams for my life! I thank you in advance for showing me your dreams and your heart! In Jesus mighty name I pray, Amen.

Things to consider:

Take a moment to pray and spend time in His presence. Write down below things that the Father has shown you about your life.

Who are your inner circle leaders?

How can you pray for them today?

....

....

WEEK 6, DAY 1

Monday

Lord, Increase My Greatness and give me Vision!

**Begin by taking a moment to stay still in God's presence.
Holy Spirit come, I turn my attention to you.**

Scripture Reading:

Psalm 71:20-21

"You, who have shown me great and severe troubles, shall revive me again, and bring me up again from the depths of the earth. You shall increase my greatness, and comfort me on every side."

Also read Psalm 73:1-17

Devotional thought:

There is a difference between followers and leaders.

A leader has great vision, helping them have great perspective and to stay on course. Vision gives you hope for the future, because without envisioning the future, the leader lacks power for the present. A leader's God-given vision is one you believe in when others cannot see its potential.

Devotional Prayer:

Thank you, Father, for every hard time you have ever allowed me to endure, for you have worked (or are working) in every one of these areas for my good. Thank you for sustaining me through every trial I've ever been through in my life. Thank you for bringing me to where I am today and for being with me always. I trust you Father, I love you, and I know that my times are in your hands.

Thank you for the vision and perspective you have inspired from within me to outwork your purpose in my life. I ask that you continue to give me your grace and power to lead in this season and every season.

Thank you for bringing me out into a wide place, a good place. Father, even though I've experienced trials, I know that you will revive me again. Father God, I ask you to fill me with your fresh fire and to let the rain of your Spirit pour into my spirit, soul and body right now. I ask you to roar over me right now and fill me with your courage and strength. I ask you to fill me with your peace, joy and power with your roar. I ask you to wake me up and fill me with more abundant life this moment. I ask you to bless me, to enlarge my territory, that your hand would be with me; that you would keep me from evil; and that you would not cause me pain. Father, increase my greatness—for Your glory. Father, increase my greatness—for your good pleasure. I ask you to increase my greatness because you love me. I ask you to make all the changes in my life that are necessary in order for me to represent you well on the earth and show the world who you really are. I ask you to make me a playground for pouring out all the good and perfect gifts that you have been yearning and craving to give me. I ask you Father to use me as a tool in your hand for the earth to be filled with the knowledge of your glory as the waters cover the sea. I declare with my own tongue that I live to give you glory. I will not forget the Lord my God, who gives me power to get wealth, and so this confirms your covenant, which you swore to my fathers! I ask you to bring me comfort and encouragement in every situation in my life, every moment of every day. Thank you, Father, for increasing me, comforting me and using my life as your playground and sandbox for pouring out your goodness on the earth! Thank you for blessing me and taking care of me so well. I give you all the glory, honour and praise! In Jesus mighty name I pray, Amen.

Things to consider:

What is your God-given vision for your business?

How can your vision impact others to glorify Father God?

Have you set goals on how you will achieve this?

Write below your thoughts/goals…

....

....

....

WEEK 6, DAY 2

Tuesday

Integrity & Excellence

**Begin by taking a moment to stay
still in God's presence.
Holy Spirit come, I turn my attention to you.**

Scripture Readings:

Psalm 72:18-19

"Blessed be the Lord God, the God of Israel, who only does wondrous things! And blessed be His glorious name forever! And let the whole earth be filled with His glory. Amen and Amen."

Psalm 78:72

"And David shepherded them with integrity of heart; with skilful hands he led them."

Devotional thought:

David was a successful leader, as he lead with integrity and diligence. He did this in two ways: with skilful and gifted hands and also with a pure heart. These are characteristics that every great and gifted Spiritual leader carries. David led with excellence through heart and skill. Having one without the other leads to disaster.

Devotional Prayer:

Father, today I praise and thank you for everything you have done and everything you are going to do. Father, I stand in awe of you! I bless you. Blessed be Your name! I bless You, Lord God Almighty! You alone are the one that does wondrous things because everything is in your hand. I ask you to continue to do amazing, wondrous things for me today and everyday.

Teach me Father how to value excellence and not settle for doing an average job. Help me to continue paying attention to detail and remaining committed to what really matters. Thank you that you have placed within me the integrity and sound ethics. Help me to continue to show genuine respect for others and to go the extra mile in everything I do, for your glory. Help me to continue to demonstrate consistency and never stop improving. I always want to give 100% and make excellence my lifestyle, because I do everything as if I am doing it unto you. I thank you for the wondrous plans you have for my life. I ask you to glorify your own name in me. I give you all the glory in my life. Father use me to make your name famous across the whole earth. Father let the earth be filled with your glory. I ask you to give me your eternal perspective and show me how I can be a part of your perfect plan to glorify Jesus across the whole earth. Thank you for allowing me to be part of your perfect plan and what you are doing around the world. I pray all of these things in the mighty name of Jesus, Amen.

Things to consider:

Take a moment to recognise the goodness of God and write down below three things you are thankful for that you have seen God's hand upon in your business.

What are the areas in your life that require some more input to show excellence in your leadership? Just like David did, we want to operate with Integrity and skill by using our heart and our creativity.

....
....
....
....
....
....
....
....
....
....

WEEK 6, DAY 3

How to Defeat the Enemy.

**Begin by taking a moment to stay
still in God's presence.
Holy Spirit come, I turn my attention to you.**

Scripture Reading:

Ephesians 6:11-17

"Put on the full armour of God, so that you can take your stand against the devil's schemes. For our struggle is not against flesh and blood, but against the rulers, against the authorities, against the powers of this dark world and against the spiritual forces of evil in the heavenly realms. Therefore put on the full armour of God so that when the day of evil comes, you may be able to stand your ground, and after you have done everything, to stand. Stand firm then, with the belt of truth buckled around your waist, with the breastplate of righteousness in place, and with your feet fitted with the readiness that comes from the gospel of peace. In addition to all this, take up the shield of faith, with which you can extinguish all the flaming arrows of the evil one. Take the helmet of salvation and the sword of the Spirit, which is the word of God."

Devotional thought:

Paul writes to his people and warns them of things that may happen through tough times and Satan's evil plans. Paul, being a good leader, doesn't show grief or despair. However, he gives them a plan of attack. He guides them not to fight in their own strength, but that only God can defeat the enemy. As you lead your people, you always want to provide them with: a plan to win, awareness of the opposition, resources they need, a plan for how to use them, and a detailed instruction guide.

Devotional Prayer:

Father, today I thank you for your powerful work in my life and your consistent love that flows through me to others. Today I choose to put on all of God's armour so that I am able to stand firm against all of the strategies of the enemy in my workplace and my business. I know that I am not fighting against flesh and blood enemies, but against evil rulers and authorities of the unseen world, against mighty powers in this dark world, and against evil spirits.

Father I put on every piece of Your armour so I will be able to resist the enemy in the time of evil. Then after the battle, I will be standing firm. I stand my ground, putting on the belt of truth. Lord, your Word is truth and it has your mighty weapons, not worldly weapons, that I use to knock down the strongholds of human reasoning and to destroy false arguments.

I put on the body armour of your righteousness, which is faith and love. On my feet, I put on the feet of readiness that comes from the Gospel of peace, so that I will be fully prepared. For Christ Jesus himself is my peace. I seek peace and pursue it with others. Father, now you have given me the task of reconciling others to you. Help me discern how to do this in the marketplace.

I hold up the shield of faith to stop all the fiery arrows of the devil. I put on Salvation as my helmet and take the sword of the Spirit, which is the Word of the Spirit. Father, I believe Your Word and speak your Word. You have given me authority over all the power of the enemy and nothing will harm me. Greater is the One who is in me than the one who is in the world.

I will pray in the Spirit at all times and on every occasion. I stay alert and I am persistent in my prayers for all believers everywhere. My qualification comes from God. He has enabled me to be a minister of His New Covenant - a Covenant not of written laws but of the Spirit who gives life. Thank you Father for Your empowering me as I wear my armour in my workplace and bring heaven to earth. In Jesus mighty name I pray, Amen.

Things to consider:

Are you prepared for spiritual battles, remembering that there are battles that can't be won with physical means, but only through spiritual means from a heavenly perspective. List the giants that need to fall and consider fasting and praying for three days. (When fasting, consider a method that is suitable to your health conditions.)

As a leader, you want to provide your people with a strategy to be successful in what they are entrusted with by giving them resources and a plan of how to use them. Write down areas that can be improved in your business/leadership.

WEEK 3, DAY 4

Thursday

God's Redemptive Work and The Leader.

**Begin by taking a moment to stay still in God's presence.
Holy Spirit come, I turn my attention to you.**

Scripture readings:

Ephesians 1:15-23

"For this reason, ever since I heard about your faith in the Lord Jesus and your love for all God's people, I have not stopped giving thanks for you, remembering you in my prayers. I keep asking that the God of our Lord Jesus Christ, the glorious Father, may give you the Spirit of wisdom and revelation so that you may know him better. I pray that the eyes of your heart may be enlightened in order that you may know the hope to which he has called you, the riches of his glorious inheritance in his holy people, and his incomparably great power for us who believe. That power is the same as the mighty strength he exerted when he raised Christ from the dead and seated him at his right hand in the heavenly realms, far above all rule and authority, power and dominion, and every name that is invoked, not only in the present age but also in the one to come. And God placed all things under his feet and appointed him to be head over everything for the church, which is his body, the fullness of him who fills everything in every way."

Devotional Thought:

Influence flows from the leader's identity. A leader in the marketplace or in their business touches the heart of their staff before they see their vision accomplished. This is by using their gifts and talents to equip people as a primary role. Accountability and authority comes with responsibility, but leaders are able to raise the bar and celebrate their fellow colleagues, even through diversity. Great leaders know how to birth unity and are able to also celebrate progressive steps of the business within the workplace. Leaders know how to make a difference.

Devotional Prayer:

Father God, I thank you for the Spirit of wisdom and revelation that is engrafted
 within me. I pray that you would make me more conscious of the precious gift
 of wisdom and revelation that you have imprinted within me. Enlighten my eyes
 so that I may see the hope that you have called me to. Show me your glory in my
 workplace. May your power fill the room and every meeting that I attend. May

your strong and tangible presence be my anchor and shield. You are my source of strength and life; you are the one that gives me courage and peace in every situation. Thank you Father for your abounding grace and love that overflows from within me. Thank you for giving me influence through my leadership, in my business and workplace. Thank you for giving me a heart of flesh so that I may be sensitive to the people I lead and be able to equip them through the sensitivity of your Spirit. Thank you for giving me the wisdom to be able to identify a moment that needs to be celebrated and a moment that needs care in my workplace and business. I pray unity within my team and my workplace so that it may grow and take progressive steps for the glory of your name. Thank you for the outpouring of blessings over my business and team because you said in your Word, that when there is unity, you command a blessing. I speak that and declare that right now. Help me to be a clear vessel and a good example of who you want me to be in the marketplace. Use me for your glory, Lord. Refine me to be the best representation of you on this earth. I pray this in Jesus mighty name, Amen!

Things to Consider:

What are the ways that you can touch the heart of the people around you?

Consider serving your people first before achieving their KPI's (Key Performance Indicators).

List the different ways that you can equip your people and those who are around you.

....

....

WEEK 6, DAY 5

Inclining my ear to God for Wisdom and Wholeness.

**Begin by taking a moment to stay
still in God's presence.
Holy Spirit come, I turn my attention to you.**

Scripture Reading:

Proverbs 4:20-27

"My son, pay attention to what I say; turn your ear to my words.
Do not let them out of your sight, keep them within your heart;
for they are life to those who find them and health to one's whole body.
Above all else, guard your heart, for everything you do flows from it. Keep your mouth free from perversity; keep corrupt talk far from your lips.

Let your eyes look straight ahead; fix your gaze directly before you. Give careful thought to the paths of your feet and be steadfast in all your ways. Do not turn to the right or to the left; keep your foot from evil."

Devotional Thought:

Strong leaders are not just leaders because of the way they were brought up, or by their culture. Strong leaders last and prosper in all they do because they base everything on principles. Principles can't not be broken.

Proverbs 4 encourages leaders to base all that they do around principles. Verses 20-27 guide us to three very important Godly things to learn from:

1. God's principles keep us on the right track.
2. God's principles shield us and keep us protected from the terror of night and the arrows that fly by day.
3. God's principles enable us to evaluate ourselves and measure where we are heading in life.

Devotional Prayer:

Thank you, Father, for your loving kindness and grace, that you want to give me wholeness and wisdom in my life.
Thank you, Father, for bringing me out of the land of Egypt to walk in all of your ways, that it may be well with my soul. Forgive me for the times I didn't incline my ears to hear your words and follow your ways. Help me to sit in your presence and enjoy it more than anything in this world. Teach me, Holy Spirit, how to pay attention to what you say. Teach me how to hold your words in my heart and

how to never lose sight of your words in my life. Thank you, Father, because you promise me wisdom, life, health and wholeness if I incline my ears to you and hear you speak into my life. Help me become more sensitive to your Holy Spirit to notice your work in my workplace and business.

I declare today that I will obey your Word and I will incline my ear to your voice. I will not follow what counsels and dictates the world. I will walk in all of the ways you have commanded me so that I may prosper. I will amend my ways and my doings according to your Word. Father, do not allow for anything to take this away from me. I thank you because your ways are good and they are a lamp unto my feet. I give you all the praise and glory, for you are good. In Jesus mighty name I pray, Amen.

Things to consider:

God's principles help build our character, direct the decisions we make and correct our lifestyle. As a Christian leader, you should consume the Word of God, evaluate God's truths over your life and through this, discover the principles that God has placed before you to guide, guard and gauge your life.

Write below the principles that Holy Spirit has stirred in your heart to help you for the next season ahead.

....

....

....

....

....

About the authors

ANDREW AND MONA HANNA are Kingdom entrepreneurs that have vast experience in life, business and ministry. Over the last 20 years they have had the opportunity to invest in multiple ventures. They believe that having passive multiple streams of income will allow you to serve and build the Kingdom of God with freedom.

Using Kingdom Biblical Principles, they have pioneered diverse investing strategies, allowing them to manage and multiply what God has entrusted them with. Andrew and Mona believe that God doesn't need our money; He needs good managers of His money.

They have seen God move supernaturally in their finance journey and carry a unique entrepreneurial anointing to release and impart God's financial provision over you, your family, and your business.

Andrew and Mona have three anointed and appointed children: Jeremiah, Bethany and Elijah. They run Kingdom Business & Supernatural Ministry and they are also Family Pastors at Horizon Church Sydney, Australia and sit on multiple ministry and business Boards. They believe in a holistic lifestyle that includes family, business and ministry. They are passionate to see Kingdom entrepreneurs achieve influence and success in the marketplace through Biblical principles. **www.kbsm.com.au**

www.ingramcontent.com/pod-product-compliance
Lightning Source LLC
Chambersburg PA
CBHW070507100426
42743CB00010B/1781